8.99

SIGHT

Sally Hewitt

This library edition published in 2016
by Quarto Library., an imprint of QEB Publishing, Inc.

6 Orchard, Lake Forest, CA 92630

© 2016 QEB Publishing,
Published by Quarto Library.,
an imprint of Quarto Publishing Group USA Inc.

Distributed in the United States and Canada by
Lerner Publisher Services
241 First Avenue North
Minneapolis, MN 55401 U.S.A.
www.lernerbooks.com

A CIP record for the book is available from the Library of Congress.

ISBN 978 1 60992 880 3

Printed in China

Publisher: Maxime Boucknooghe
Editorial Director: Victoria Garrard
Art Director: Miranda Snow
Series Editor: Claudia Martin
Series Designer: Bruce Marshall
Photographer: Michael Wicks
Consultant: Kristina Routh

Picture credits
t = top, b = bottom, c = center, l = left, r = right,
fc = front cover

Alamy 18r Paul Doyle, 19 Elizabeth Whiting & Associates
Corbis 5r Ariel Skelley, 6t Ralph A. Clevenger, 7 Christoph Wilhelm, 18l Julio Donoso/Sygma, 12 and 18r Gabe Palmer, 17b Roy Morsch, 10t Roger Ressmeyer
Getty Images 5t E. Dygas/Taxi, 10b Jeffrey Sylvester/Taxi, 14 SteveCole/Photographers Choice, 16t Michael Denora/The Image Bank, 16b David Hume Kennerly/Reportage, 17t UHB Trust/Stone
Shutterstock fc Jacek Chabraszewski/bestv/ aimy 27feb/Richard Peterson, 8r Tefi, shutterstock 10t raysay, 13l NikolayN, 15r tanatat, 17r Darren Baker

Words in **bold** can be found in the glossary on page 22.

Contents

Look around

You have five main senses that give you information about the world around you.

The fives senses are sight, touch, smell, taste, and hearing.

This book is about sight.

◀ Your sight helps you to read your favorite books.

◀ Your sight helps you
to cross the road safely.

Your sense of
sight lets you see
colors, shapes, and
moving objects.

Look around you.
What can you see?

▶ Your sight helps you
choose clothes to wear.

Light to see

Eyes are the part of the body that you see with. You need light to see.

▶ When your eyes are shut, light can't get in so you can't see.

Iris

Pupil

The colored circle in your eye is the **iris**.

The black circle in the iris is called the **pupil**. A pupil is a gap in your iris that lets light into you eyes.

When it is dark, your pupils get bigger to let in more light. When it is very bright, your pupils get smaller to stop too much light hurting your eyes.

Activity

Close your eyes for a minute then open them and look in a mirror. Your pupils should look bigger!

Look out of the window in daylight, then look in a mirror. Your pupils should look smaller!

How your eyes work

Light bounces off the objects around you, then enters your eyes. Your **lens** uses the light to make a picture.

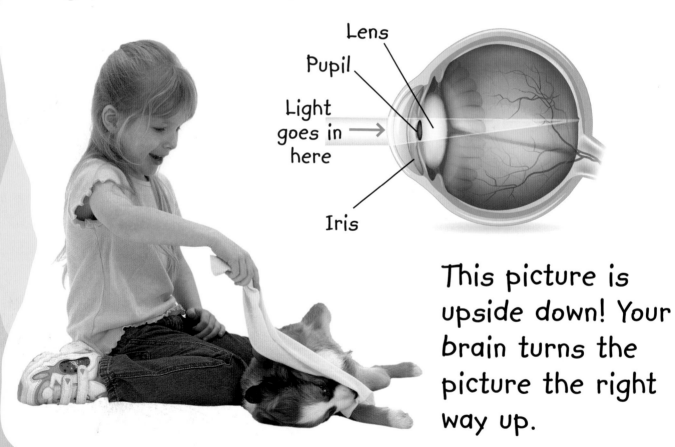

Lens

Pupil

Light goes in here

Iris

This picture is upside down! Your brain turns the picture the right way up.

Your eyes can see colors clearly in bright light. When it's darker, most colors look gray.

What colors can you see in this picture?

▶ If you shut the curtains or turn off the light, you might see the shapes of this picture, but the colors will look gray.

Why two eyes?

Having two eyes helps you to tell how far away things are.

Each of your eyes gives a slightly different picture of the world. Your brain combines the two pictures so you can see.

◀ Your two eyes move together.

▶ A chameleon can look up with one eye and down with the other eye at the same time!

Activity

Try this activity to find out how useful it is to have two eyes.

- Hold a pen out in front of you.

- Close your left eye, then your right eye. Does the position of the pen change slightly?

- Now, with both eyes open, try to put a top on the pen.

- Then shut one eye and try to put the top on the pen. Is it harder this time?

Look and learn

You can learn all sorts of things by looking carefully.

Look at these children. Can you tell if they are happy or sad? Can you guess where they might be going?

What else can you tell about them just by looking?

Your eyes send messages to your brain about what you see.

Activity

Look carefully at these pictures then cover them up.

Ball   Plate   Flower   Rubber duck

What can you remember?
How many things are there?
What color is the ball?
What color is the plate?
What other details can you remember?

Bigger and smaller

We also use lenses made of curved pieces of glass or plastic to help us see. They can make things look bigger, smaller, nearer, or farther away.

◀ A planet looks like a tiny dot in the night sky. A **telescope** makes it look nearer.

A **magnifying glass** makes things look bigger. The lens is thicker in the middle making it curved.

▶ The pattern of your fingerprint can be seen under a magnifying glass lens.

Activity

These two objects have been magnified. Can you tell what they are?

▶ This is juicy and sweet.

◀ This is for your hair.

Wearing glasses

Glasses have special lenses which help people to see more clearly.

◀ Far-sighted people need glasses to help them see things close up, such as when you read a book.

▶ Near-sighted people need glasses to see things that are far away.

◀ Contact lenses are put straight onto the eye. Just like glasses, they help people to see more clearly.

Sunglasses help to protect your eyes in bright sunlight. They stop harmful rays from the sun entering your eyes.

Being blind

People who are blind learn to get more information from their other senses.

You can tell if a person is happy or sad from the sound of their voice.

◀ Blind children learn using their sense of touch.

▶ Blind people can learn to read Braille. This is a series of raised dots which form words.

Why should a room be kept tidy for someone who can't see?

Blind people can find things easier if they are always kept in the same place.

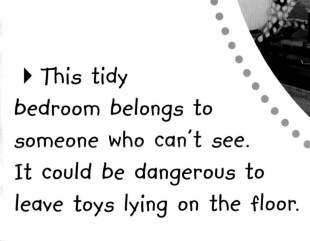

▶ This tidy bedroom belongs to someone who can't see. It could be dangerous to leave toys lying on the floor.

Trick your eyes

You can trick your eyes into seeing things differently.

◀ Look at this picture. Can you see a rabbit, a duck, or both?

This picture is called an optical illusion. It looks like one thing but it could be another!

A film looks like one moving picture. It is actually lots of still pictures moving in sequence very quickly!

Activity

Make your own moving film!

- Draw 5 pictures in a sequence, like these:

- Put the pages in order and flick them quickly from front to back to see the figure move. Add more drawings to your sequence to make it longer.

GLOSSARY

Eyes

Your eyes are shaped like small, round balls. You can see only the front part of your eyes.

Iris

The colored part of your eye is called the iris. People have different colored irises, such as green, blue, and brown.

Lens

The lens in your eye helps you to see things. Lenses in glasses can help make things look bigger or smaller.

Light

Light comes from the Sun, electric lights, or fire. Light helps you to see. Your pupils let light in or keep light out.

Magnifying glass

A magnifying glass has a curved glass or plastic lens. It makes things look bigger.

Pupil

The black circle in your eye is called the pupil. Your pupils are gaps in your irises which open and close to let light in or keep light out.

Telescope

A telescope uses curved glass or plastic lens to make things that are far away look closer.

INDEX

NEXT STEPS

* Play games that involve looking carefully. You could ask your child to study a picture, then take it away and ask them questions about it. What can they remember? *I-Spy* and *Pairs* are good games for looking and remembering.

* Collect things that children can discuss, such as pages from a children's clothes catalog, well-known paintings, flowers, or pieces of material. Ask the children to describe them. Talk about what they like or dislike about the look of them, such as the color or the shape.

* Talk about protecting your eyes. Never look directly at the Sun. Sunglasses help to protect your eyes from bright sunlight. Goggles help to protect your eyes in a swimming pool.

* Look at pictures of animals and talk about their eyes. Are they on the front or the sides of their heads? Are their eyes big or small? Do the animals have to see at night or underwater? Do they use their eyes for hunting?

* Explain that we *see* when light bounces off objects and goes into our eyes. Try looking at a plant or painting in bright light, in shadow, and then in a darkened room. Talk about how the amount of light changes what you can *see*.

* Gather a group of pictures of people from magazines or the internet. Guess which is the most common eye color in the pictures. Make a block graph recording the eye colors and compare the result with the children's guesses.